{SANCTUARY}

{SANCTUARY}

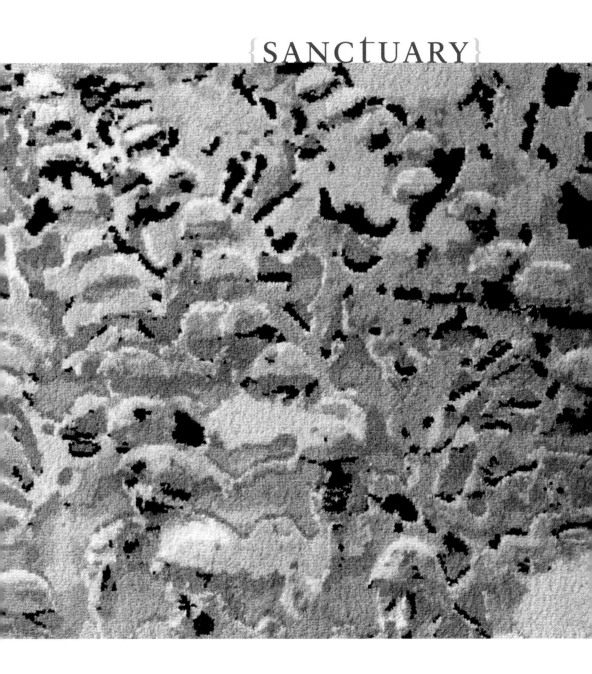

{ FOR-SITE FOUNDATION }

Established in 2003, the FOR-SITE Foundation is dedicated to the creation, understanding, and presentation of art about place. Our exhibitions and commissions, artist residencies, and education programs are based in the belief that art can inspire fresh thinking and important dialogue about our natural and cultural environment.

FOR-SITE Foundation
2 Marina Blvd., Building C
San Francisco, CA 94123
www.for-site.org

ISBN 978-0-692-94977-1

Printed in the United States of America

9 8 7 6 5 4 3 2 1

Contents

01 Mona **Hatoum** { B. 1952, LEBANON }

02 Sanaz **Mazinani** { B. 1978, IRAN }

03 Jamal **Cyrus** { B. 1973, UNITED STATES }

04 **Uman** { B. 1980, SOMALIA }

05 Hayv **Kahraman** { B. 1981, IRAQ }

06 Ranu **Mukherjee** { B. 1966, UNITED STATES }

07 John **Akomfrah** { B. 1957, GHANA }

08 Thaier **Helal** { B. 1967, SYRIA }

09 Shiva **Ahmadi** { B. 1975, IRAN }

10 Adel **Abidin** { B. 1973, IRAQ }

11 Marcos Ramírez **ERRE** { B. 1961, MEXICO }

12 Susan **Hefuna** { B. 1962, GERMANY }

13 Ana Teresa **Fernández** { B. 1981, MEXICO }

14 Cornelia **Parker** { B. 1956, UNITED KINGDOM }

15 Ala **Ebtekar** { B. 1978, UNITED STATES }

16 Emily **Jacir** { B. 1972, PALESTINE }

17 Sandow **Birk** { B. 1962, UNITED STATES }

18 Alfredo **Jaar** { B. 1956, CHILE }

19 Hamra **Abbas** { B. 1976, KUWAIT }

20 Arwa **Abouon** { B. 1982, LIBYA }

21 Diana **Al-Hadid** { B. 1981, SYRIA }

22 Hank Willis **Thomas** { B. 1976, UNITED STATES }

23 Ammar **al-Beik** { B. 1972, SYRIA }

24 Nicholas **Galanin** { B. 1979, UNITED STATES }

25 **Ai** Weiwei { B. 1957, CHINA }

26 Tammam **Azzam** { B. 1980, SYRIA }

27 Mohammad **Bozorgi** { B. 1978, IRAN }

28 Aimé **Mpane** { B. 1968, DEMOCRATIC REPUBLIC OF THE CONGO }

29 Shirazeh **Houshiary** { B. 1955, IRAN }

30 Rashid **Rana** { B. 1968, PAKISTAN }

31 Miguel Angel **Ríos** { B. 1943, ARGENTINA }

32 Sherin **Guirguis** { B. 1974, EGYPT }

33 Julio César **Morales** { B. 1966, MEXICO }

34 Jeffrey **Gibson** { B. 1972, UNITED STATES }

35 Meleko **Mokgosi** { B. 1981, BOTSWANA }

36 Brendan **Fernandes** { B. 1979, KENYA }

Exhibition **Overview**

{ FOR-SITE FOUNDATION }

THE NOTION OF SANCTUARY—both physical and psychological—has been fundamental in shaping a sense of selfhood and social identity throughout human history. From the Middle Ages to today, it has signified refuge and protection, as well as sacred ground. But in an era of increasing global migration and rising nationalism, the right to safe haven is under threat: racial, ethnic, national, and cultural differences have become seemingly intractable divisions, prompting us to insulate and isolate ourselves—to mistrust the "other" and succumb to misdirected fear. In this climate, the need for compassion is greater than ever.

In response to the shifting sense of safety and perceived loss of sacred space around the world, we invited 36 contemporary artists from 21 countries to reflect on ideas of sanctuary and create designs for four-by-six-foot wool rugs, woven by hand in Lahore, Pakistan. Installed on the floor in Fort Mason Chapel—a decommissioned, nondenominational gathering and worship space—the artworks call to mind traditional prayer rugs, but they transcend religious connotations, encompassing thoughtful perspectives on cultural identity, sense of place, and belonging. The designs are spectacularly varied, echoing the great diversity in the artists' heritages, philosophies, and personal histories—many of which include experiences as migrants and refugees. In the artists' hands, utilitarian objects become powerful sites of reflection, and the artists' individual points of view unveil universal themes.

Historically and traditionally, rugs are a medium for cultural expression: They embody the geography and values of the people who make them. Their symbols, patterns, and materials reveal deeply personal narratives—stories of history, place, purpose, and faith. As a prayer rug defines a sacred space and mediates between the material and the spiritual, the rugs in *Sanctuary* create a distinct material boundary that encloses a safe space for contemplation, introspection, and interpretation. This space of the rug is necessarily mobile, temporary—able to be rolled up, transported, and deployed as needed.

The rugs on view are meant to be appreciated by touch as well as sight. Visitors are encouraged to remove shoes and walk, sit, and recline on the artworks—to quietly contemplate our shared humanity and this space of sanctuary. ⌐

ABOUT FORT MASON CHAPEL *Built in 1942, Fort Mason Chapel employs the standardized floor plan and interior design assigned to all US Army posts in the early 20th century. However, its Mission Revival exterior—with red-tile roof, bell tower, unadorned stucco, and inset doorway—reveals the contemporaneous interest in the historic architecture of the Western missions. Post chapels served as nondenominational places of worship and familiar gathering spots for servicemen and -women, who were often stationed far from home and family. As such, they provided valuable sources of comfort and uplift during difficult times.*

The weaving techniques used to create the rugs in *Sanctuary* follow centuries-old traditions that some scholars believe originated in the Indus Valley region around present-day Lahore, Pakistan. Executing the elaborate designs for which the region is known requires years of training, and a laborious process that can span months for a single rug.

Each rug begins with a design translated onto graph paper at full scale. Next, the design is recorded in Taalim, an ancient language that provides instructions for the rug's knots and colors. Yarn is hand-dyed in batches—the rugs for *Sanctuary* required 102 different colors—then woven through the base fibers, or warp, on the loom. The completed rug is washed and allowed to dry in the sun, which gives the natural fibers a sheen that cannot be attained by other drying methods. Finally, the pile is sheared, and the warp given a finishing trim.

PRECEDING PAGE Removing Hank Willis Thomas's rug from the loom.

BELOW Knotting techniques vary according to tribe and geography of origin. Here, the weaver works on Hank Willis Thomas's *Sanctuary* design.

BELOW Dying yarn is a multifaceted process tailored for each rug.

OVERLEAF The equipment and techniques employed in rug-making have changed little over the centuries, as exemplified by Susan Hefuna's *Sanctuary* rug on the loom.

On the Reality of Sanctuaries
and the Fiction of Borders

[REBECCA SOLNIT]

1.

BORDERS HAVE ALWAYS been described as if they were real demarcations in the land. When I was a child, and people talked about the Iron Curtain separating the communist East from the capitalist West, I pictured an enormous cyclone fence that crossed a continent—and of course there was no such structure. But I floated down the United States–Mexico border in the late 1990s; the Rio Grande flows through the middle of New Mexico until it suddenly becomes what divides Texas from Chihuahua—except that it doesn't. In many places, the river is so shallow that cows walk across it as birds crisscross overhead. A river is where thirsty life gathers, and of course, for birds there are no borders.

Those who view border crossers as transgressive think of the border as an important, natural, and authentic thing. The operative metaphor here is "the nation as a body." I've always thought that there must be a lot of male, heterosexual, homophobic anxiety underlying this notion that the body must not be penetrated. It's similar to the disease metaphor that's been applied to Jews and other immigrants, who are seen as dirty, or as viruses that might infect the body. But anybody who thinks their body is impenetrable should stop breathing for five minutes and get back to us. Bodies are interfused with the world and inseparable from the world around them, unless they're dead bodies.

When you're in the wilderness, you realize that the notion of a border doesn't mean anything. There is no line separating California from Nevada, either, though you might find a sign welcoming you to the next state. Borders themselves are a fiction, and every body is in motion. The idea that some bodies are in motion and need to be arrested, literally and metaphorically, while other bodies are stable, is complicated, unless you're referring to indigenous peoples, such as the indigenous Pueblo people, who actually live on the Rio Grande in New Mexico and have been there for a thousand years or more.

Seeing the border as a river was just seeing that there is no real border. We can build walls and have men with guns to keep people from moving, but the only natural division in the world, really, is between the land and the sea, and that changes all the time—at high tide and low tide and riptide and everything in between. And climate change will redraw the coastlines all over the world; that's one border transgression I could do without.

The monarch butterfly is a species that, in its life cycle, exists on both sides of what, for butterflies, is not a border. The great womb of the monarch butterflies—their southernmost point, where they hibernate and generate the next generation—is in the highland forests of Mexico, and from there they migrate (in multiple generations) all the way to the Canadian border, and then back. (West of the Sierra Nevada they just come to the coast for their overwintering spots.) In fact, all flying things have a wonderful way of refusing the legitimacy and authority and even the reality of borders. The DREAMers—those young, undocumented immigrants protected from deportation by President Barack Obama's Deferred Action for Childhood Arrivals (DACA) policy—have taken up the monarch butterfly as a powerful symbol of their own transformation, and of the beauty of a life without borders.

National borders are often crossed by those in search of sanctuary. In the early 1980s, when an influx of refugees traveled north from Central America to the United States to escape the civil wars in places like Nicaragua and Guatemala, they would arrive and take refuge from the state's deportation machine in churches, living there for extended periods, as some of them had done in Central America. The Sanctuary Movement—and the notion of sanctuary cities—evolved in response to this moment, when Catholic and Protestant churches played an important role in giving shelter to refugees, reviving the old idea of churches as sanctuaries from the state that dates back to the Middle Ages. Churches' willingness to serve as sanctuaries hinged on a sense that secular law has no jurisdiction over the church, as if the church has its own law. This notion suggests a separation of church and state that is different than the one people usually refer to. This legacy continues into the present, as churches continue to provide safe harbor for those in need.

Part of what's so troublesome about the narratives around undocumented immigrants is that the US government has often created the trouble that these immigrants are hoping to find refuge from. The United States took children who arrived here as refugees in the 1980s and were corrupted by our own inner-city gangs and drug economies and sent them back to places like Honduras and El Salvador, where they created a great deal of the extreme violence that's now driving a new generation of refugees here. The drug wars in Mexico are caused, in no small part, by US drug consumption and US weapons that are being smuggled southward as drugs are being smuggled northward. If everyone in America gave up cocaine and heroin and methamphetamine and the marijuana that's not a domestic product, the cartels would evaporate. People claim that immigrants are bringing danger into our "pure" country, but we created much of the danger that they're fleeing, and they're fleeing it by coming here.

There is another kind of obsession with contamination, with borders and segregation and exclusion, that stems from people who fear that they'll become impure if they associate with people who do not think exactly like they do. But when you have common ground with people about something truly important, you must put aside differences and embrace what you have in common. A sanctuary can become toxic when it becomes a gated community, where those inside can't deal with people who aren't like themselves. A cosmopolitan sanctuary is one in which we don't need to be segregated to be safe, don't need to be separate from people who are different.

One of the big arguments in this country right now is between those people fearing that their purity is contaminated by difference and those who have adopted a cosmopolitan model, in which difference coexists fruitfully and is viewed as something that energizes us. The latter is an urban narrative, and right now we're in a civil war that pits the suburban and rural against the urban. President Donald Trump is from New York—a cosmopolitan city that thrives on diversity, a city that's nonwhite majority and 37 percent immigrant—but he discovered that segregation and purity were products that he could market. He's given power and voice to a dangerous part of the population who believes that.

Trump understands that enemies are very useful organizing principles, and that they can be used to create a narrative around "us and them" that energizes the politics of hate. This is not an entirely new situation. When the Cold War ended, one wondered where the next enemy might be found, who might be tossed into the breach to supply what the great Edward Said named as "the other." Immigrants have played this role at other times in US history, from the Know-Nothing Party and anti-Irish and anti-German movements of the 1840s and '50s to the anti-Chinese sentiment, which dates back to the late 19th century and was a terrible curse in San Francisco, resulting in the anti-Chinese riots in 1877. Sometimes these fears fuel laws, such as the policies that deported anarchist writer and activist Emma Goldman back to Russia after World War I, and the Immigration Act of 1924, which targeted Japanese Americans.

We hear so much now from certain segments of the white heterosexual Christian population, for whom poor people, gay people, non-Christian people, and nonwhite people are the other they want purged. In fact, this raises a question for everyone: what is your otherness, and how do you relate to it? One could say that the conflict in this country is the result of competing visions of sanctuary—one cosmopolitan and inclusive, the other based on exclusion—and a question of whether these visions can be reconciled.

Inclusive sanctuaries become possible when we unite in our efforts to provide safety for others. In July 2017, at the beach in Panama City, Florida, a woman, her two young sons, and the boys' grandmother were caught in a deadly riptide. In response, 80 people rushed into the water and, holding on to one another, formed a human chain to rescue the family from drowning. No one in the group of all ages, races, and genders was strong enough to swim out alone and bring the family back, but together they created a bridge that spanned the distance from the shoreline to survival.

Inclusive sanctuaries resist orthodoxies. During the 2011 uprising in Cairo's Tahrir Square, as progovernment forces threatened to attack protestors, Muslims stood to protect the Christians at prayer, and Christians stood to protect Muslims during their time of worship. Armed with rocks and a sense of solidarity, members of each religious group used their bodies to create a human shield, the walls of a refuge that kept others safe.

Borders are where the liminal sometimes becomes monstrous and bureaucratic and authoritarian, but sanctuaries have their own liminality, serving as bridges between worlds. In Reza Aslan's book *Zealot: The Life and Times of Jesus of Nazareth*, Aslan describes the First Temple in Jerusalem as a bustling, commercialized place with enormous animal sacrifices. It contained what was called the Holy of Holies, the inner-sanctum where God dwelt, whose threshold only the high priest could cross. Once a year, he had to tie a rope around his waist before entering. This way, if the high priest died while atoning for the community's sins, they could drag him out without defiling the sanctuary by stepping inside to remove his corpse.

There are other spaces that only certain people should enter— sanctuaries that are by necessity based on exclusion, such as domestic violence shelters. At some point in the future, hopefully not far from now, people will say, "They were so barbaric and brutish in that age that the country was covered in sanctuaries for women and children to hide from the violence of men." We need domestic violence shelters until we don't have domestic violence, but the long-term goal is to make them unnecessary.

During a conversation around the quincentennial of Christopher Columbus's arrival in the Americas, which reframed the linked continents as a sanctuary that was violated by Europe, there was a panel discussion with a Catholic priest, an indigenous person, and Malcolm Margolin, the scholar, supporter of Native Californians, and former publisher of Heyday Books. Malcolm was talking about sacred Native American places in California, where a god is believed to reside in a particular spring or mountain and nowhere else; if you're an indigenous person exiled from the site, or it's destroyed, you're spiritually bereft. And the Catholic priest said something that I found so powerful: he drew a parallel between this and the destruction of the First Temple by the Romans, and the subsequent expulsion and exile of the Jews, which meant that they no longer had a holy place. They had to disperse, and so the diasporas began. Christians and Jews protected themselves against the vulnerability linked to a geographically rooted spirituality by creating portable religions that were no longer dependent on place—something echoed in the tradition of the prayer rug.

We're in a culture that valorizes and fetishizes and obsesses about private love, which is erotic and familiar and domestic and material—all the things that can happen inside a home. These are the subjects that psychology and therapy have tended to deal with. But when you exit that space, you're a citizen in the world, and your loves may include civil society, democracy, intellectual and spiritual ideals, a relationship to place and to the nonhuman world and to institutions. I love the idea of sanctuary as a kind of home, but then when do you go out into the world? You have a sanctuary, but ideally, it's a place you can exit. Ideally, you are not so hunted or threatened or fragile—or so demonized or rendered illegal—that you can't leave the sanctuary.

The tragedy of homelessness is life without sanctuary; the tragedy of prisoners is life without circulation. We have greatly multiplied the number of people in both categories in the last three decades. The good life, at its simplest, is when you have a shelter you can leave and return to, when you can have both public and private life. The homeless have no space in which to withdraw. Some religious organizations have worked to invite people in. One of the best examples in San Francisco is our beloved friend Father Louis Vitale, the former parish priest of St. Boniface in the Tenderloin and a great radical activist, who has been arrested for civil disobedience so many times he jokes that he only puts his collar on for such occasions. Years ago Father Vitale opened up St. Boniface as a place where people can sleep, and they call it sacred sleep. Mental illness, among other things, can erupt when people are sleep-deprived, and those without homes may never feel safe where they're trying to get rest. Father Vitale invited people to seek repose in the pews, and between and behind them. When I visited, the church was resonant with the sounds of low snores and the rasping, even breathing of the sleepers. The church provides other things, like foot washing and clean socks, but what it's really doing is offering a sanctuary to those who have none.

2.

INSIDE GRACE CATHEDRAL, on top of Nob Hill in San Francisco, there is a labyrinth, a replica of the one laid into the floor of a 13th-century gothic cathedral in Chartres, France. The labyrinth in San Francisco is a kind of sacred space, a sanctuary within a sanctuary. I remember walking it and realizing that we talk so much about walking into labyrinths, but you don't stay there. There's also an outward journey: you gain something that you take with you when you re-enter the world. A pilgrimage ends, and then you return. For some people, this journey is a daily one, happening each time they kneel on their prayer rugs; for others, it corresponds to a weekly visit to a church. But we are all in motion, moving in and out of our sanctuaries. What's the return journey from a sanctuary? It's just back out into the world.

In Buddhism, one of the credo statements—often called the Three Jewels—is, "I take refuge in the Buddha, the Sangha, and the Dharma." The Dharma is the body of teachings, the Sangha is the community, and the Buddha is the Buddha. Together, they provide a wonderful sense that these form a stronghold from which you can move freely through the world. In other traditions, there can be a sense that you're a miserable sinner who needs to repent or purify yourself. But Buddhism teaches us that you already have, some-where inside, Buddha-nature—a kind of wisdom, a calm, a con-nectedness, which is the opposite of loneliness and confusion. We have all this busy surface clutter, but if you can still it, maybe you can find the sanctuary.

Many of us think that sanctuary is something to search for, another form of the Western myth of the quest for the Holy Grail. But like the path of the labyrinth, the journey is ultimately circular, return-ing us to ourselves. I recall, at the age of 13, seeing a performance of the German dramatist Bertolt Brecht's play *Life of Galileo*, which tells the story of the astronomer's heretical discovery, through careful observation of the heavens, that the earth is not the center of the universe. Such a rearrangement of the Ptolemaic model had immense spiritual consequences. When Galileo's colleague, the more conventional Sagrado, asks him, "Where is God in your universe?" the rogue answers, finally, "In us or nowhere."

Years ago, the artist Lewis DeSoto told me, when I used the word *sacred* while writing about some of the places where he's made work, that to call something "sacred" is to imply that everything else is nonsacred, is profane. If I recall correctly, he preferred the idea that some places had intensified and particular power, but their power wasn't based on exclusion or separation. The European tradition loves its binaries—the sacred and profane, us and them, the pure and the impure—and organizes itself around them. But the idea that some places had concentrations of power and that others were more diffuse, or that some places were doors and some were walls, helps us to imagine other spiritual geographies.

Perhaps when we speak of a sanctuary, what we are referring to is a concentration of beneficence, where you can safely commune. By separating yourself from what troubles you, you can then connect to your own power, and finally to the powers in the world that elevate you, that strengthen you, that you work with, that you engage with— your values, your ideals, your institutions, and your communities. ⬭

ABOUT THE AUTHOR *San Francisco writer, historian, and activist Rebecca Solnit is the author of 20 books about geography, community, art, politics, hope, and feminism, and most recently, the essay collection* The Mother of All Questions *and (with Joshua Jelly-Schapiro and a cast of thousands)* Nonstop Metropolis: A New York City Atlas. *She is a contributing editor to* Harper's, *where she is the first woman to regularly write the Easy Chair column (founded in 1851).*

Sanctuaries have always been the foundations upon which we rebuild our communities and ourselves. At a point in history characterized by mass migration and a sweeping wave of xenophobia, however, our sanctuaries sometimes seem as fragile as those who seek them—yet they continue to flourish. The map following brings together a diverse sampling of San Francisco's many sanctuaries—places of refuge, solace, contemplation, and celebration—giving equal weight to the practical and the poetic, the subversive and the sublime. Services and shelters for recent immigrants and those in need of housing can be found here, alongside an urban corridor where endangered butterflies are thriving. Twin Peaks Tavern—the first gay bar in the country with plate-glass windows—proves that a refuge is not always a hiding place, although it must be for those seeking to shield themselves from domestic violence. Places of worship—particularly those that have welcomed the city's refugees—stand beside secular temples of the imagination. A hexagonal room filled with Agnes Martin's delicate, abstract paintings invites transcendence, while a curving ribbon of eucalyptus—Andy Goldsworthy's *Wood Line*—guides visitors through a shaded grove on a journey both outward and inward. This map is an invitation to traverse the city's salvations, to cross the thresholds of its spiritual geography. And what is the trek that marks the return from a sanctuary? It's a trip back out into the world, renewed.

{SANCtUARY}

N
W E
S

0   1 mile

0   1 kilometer

A sampling of

San Francisco's

many places of

refuge, solace,

contemplation,

and celebration

—the practical

and the poetic,

the subversive

and the sublime

Golden Gate Bridge

101

Veterans

PRESIDIO

Lincoln

1

California

Clement

Congregation Beth Sholom

Park Presidio

Geary

The Camera Obscura

Point Lobos

48th

25th

15th

Balboa

Fulton

GOLDEN GATE PARK

St. John of God

Lincoln

15th

Irving

Seventh Avenue
Presbyterian Church

Judah

9th

7th

5th

16th

14th

Kirkham

Lawton

Moraga

Great Highway

46th

Noriega

Ortega

The Green Hairstreak
Butterfly Corridor

Quintara

Rivera

Santiago

1

Taraval

Pacific Ocean

Portola

Sunset

35

Sloat

19th

Ocean

Skyline

Lake

Merced

Holloway

Lake Merced

Juniper Serra

1

John Muir

Brotherhood

35

San Francisco Bay

San Francisco SafeHouse
(confidential location)

Andy Goldsworthy's *Wood Line*

Musée Mécanique

The Wave Organ

Diego Rivera's *The Making of a Fresco Showing the Building of a City*

Fort Mason Chapel

Grace Cathedral Labyrinth

Marina

Scott

Bay

Francisco

Taylor

Jones

Leavenworth

Columbus

Sansome

Embarcadero

Bay Bridge

80

Lombard

Union

Broadway

Van Ness

Hyde

Larkin

Montgomery

Kearny

Grant

Buddha's Universal Church

Diego Rivera's *Allegory of California*

Washington

California

Pine

Bush

Sutter

Taylor

Powell

4th

Glide Memorial
Church Walk-In Center

Refugee Transitions

The Agnes Martin Room | SFMOMA

Alsabeel Masjid Noor Al-Islam Mosque

Islamic Society of San Francisco

Swords to Plowshares

101

Divisadero

Fillmore

Presidio

Lyon

Swedenborgian Church

Masjid Al-Tawheed Mosque

St. Boniface Catholic Church

St. Ignatius Catholic Church

St. Agnes Church

San Francisco
Zen Center

Geary

O'Farrell

Ellis

Golden Gate

McAllister

101

Market

Mission

8th

9th

Folsom

7th

Howard

6th

5th

Bryant

Brannan

3rd

80

Multi-Service Center South

The Sanctuary

La Casa de las Madres

Arriba Juntos

Masonic

Fell

Oak

Haight

Fulton

Page

Laguna

14th

15th

16th

17th

18th

Church

Dolores

Guerrero

Valencia

Mission

17th

TWIN
PEAKS

Market

Castro

Portola

S Van Ness

Folsom

Harrison

Bryant

Potrero

22nd

101

280

3rd

Mission Neighborhood
Resource Center

Refugee Medical Clinic | San
Francisco General Hospital

24th

The Women's Building

Jubilee Immigration Advocates

Cesar Chavez

United Council of
Human Services

Mission Dolores Cemetery |
Native American Burial Ground

Twin Peaks Tavern

Mission Blue Butterfly Habitat

Diego Rivera's *Pan
American Unity Mural*

Benny Bufano's *St.
Francis of the Guns*

Islamic Center
of San Francisco

San Francisco Muslim
Community Center

Andover

Cortland

Crescent

Silver

Cargo

Evans

3rd

Van Dyke

Jennings

Ingalls

Monterey

280

San Jose

Ocean

Mission

Persia

Russia

Mansell

Alemany

Geneva

Bayshore

101

{ IS THERE A PLACE TO APPROACH? AND SPREAD A CARPET? —SOHRAB SEPEHRI, IRANIAN POET }

Reorienting the Gaze

{ MINOO MOALLEM }

ORIENTAL AND PERSIAN hand-knotted carpets are art objects, crafts, and commodities. They come in different shapes and colors. They are in homes, universities, mosques, and museums. They are on the ground and the walls and are used as ornaments, furniture items, sacred objects, and war memorials. They are all over, horizontally and vertically, as viewers gaze up and down at them. Indeed, the story of carpets as art objects, things, and commodities since colonial modernity crosses the boundaries of various countries, cultures, historical periods, and academic disciplines. It registers multiple encounters culturally and aesthetically, along with myriad border crossings. While carpets are classified, categorized, and branded as unique to specific regions, nations, and localities, the carpet design is perhaps the most enduring representation of a hybrid assemblage of symbols and signs, as well as texts and textures, from various cultures—from Central and South Asia to East and West Asia (or the Middle East).

Perspectivism and vision are central to modernist painting, in which the optic eye is invited to look in a particular direction. However, to look at an Oriental carpet calls for reorienting the gaze. The carpet does not follow modern regimes of vision as the object of one's gaze in front of the viewer. Its location is usually underneath one's feet. The haptic touch of the feet and the body sensation are inseparable from the visual pleasures of looking at a carpet. In fact, a good-quality carpet goes against the logic of consumerism and disposability since a prevalent idea is that the more you step on a carpet, the more precious it becomes. Looking at a carpet disarranges modernist perspectivism and its separation of high culture from popular culture, redirecting the spectator's gaze toward the material objects of everyday life. The anonymity of most weavers and carpet designers hardly fits the notion of the genius artist of modernity, and calls for a radically different appreciation of art and its aesthetic pleasures.

Carpet composition converges with miniature painting, mosaic work, poetry, and architectural design. There is no beginning and no end to these convergences. One starts as the other ends. Things are in endless motion. The external and the internal reality merge with each other to create the carpet. In improvised compositions, this may reflect poetry, the local stories, the weavers' sensibilities, and spatial-aesthetic receptiveness, which reflect the eventfulness of the carpet. The body, the loom, space, and everyday life merge with each other in the carpet's expression of difference as the singularity.

As art, the Oriental carpet has had a more ambiguous identity, given its categorization as a furniture item. Carpets are depicted as either "primitive art" or art objects belonging to the past in the Orientalist discourse. The oldest ones are museumized as part of the "Islamic art and civilization" sections of European and US museums. Most of the time, they are displayed as things of the past, as goods from a civilization that does not exist anymore. Even as furniture items, carpets have been poorly categorized.

While produced at specific locations, the carpet is an object that moves around quite often, an object as important as a boat or a ship—"a floating piece of space," in Michel Foucault's terms, in our modern imagination. It connects different worlds: the emotional and the material, the private and the public, and those of consumption and production, the built environment and imaginary landscape, and labor and commodity. The carpet moves in space, yet its localization continually integrates a form of extension, or a relation to other sites, going beyond emplacement or being set in place.

As a portable object of everyday life, a carpet moves from one place to another, spatializing time as an eternal garden, a sacred object, a mnemonic device, and a techno-romantic landscape. The carpet also creates a phantasmatic landscape by depicting the infinite garden of paradise and the eternal tree of life. The carpet can express the imaginary landscape of plants, animals, sky, clouds, and colors. Such potential for the territorialization of space transcends the modern separation of culture and nature, and creates a new relationship to desire, a relationship that may create more perplexity than longing in the interests of imperialism, nationalism, and consumerism. Combining modernist genres of art, including naturalism, with vernacular designs, themes, and colors is indeed the insignia of postmodern forms of hybridity and *métissage*. In other words, carpets are not only remnants of a moment of closure in capitalist commodity circulation and its regimes of ownership, identity, and security in the transnational context of trade and commerce but also material objects provoking other forms of cultural desires and pleasures.

The prayer carpet is one of the most notable among objects that display Muslim architectural design regulating and aestheticizing time and space. It is used for both public and private places, such as mosques, homes, and holy shrines, and is produced as a small rug that spatializes prayer. It is a carpet with a hybrid design that brings together the symbols of pre-Islamic traditions celebrating life and Islamic universalism, directing all prayers toward Kaaba in Mecca. The use of an arched doorway or *mihrab* as a central organizing compositional motif replicates the *qibla*, which channels and guides believers in the direction of Mecca as they engage in the performance of the prayer or *namaz*. The carpet's aesthetics of sensitivity encompass the ethical experience of praying.

As mnemonic objects, carpets carry the stories of a specific locality as they track the happenings that took place at the time of the weaving, not only in some of the figurative designs such as the *gabbeh* (handwoven rugs mostly made by nomadic women where sometimes stories are interwoven in the pattern of the carpets) but also in the uniqueness of every imperfect knot that leaves the eventful trace of the haptic memory of the hands and bodies at the loom.

Carpets take on a different meaning for diasporic communities. Memories of home and homeland or expressions of belonging are conveyed through tactility and the sensation of one's consumptive practices, whether related to home decoration, fashion, or culinary habits. In this context, carpets become a spatialized site of one's identity, since stepping on them daily is a reminder of one's sensory connection to another place—somewhere far from the United States but in proximity to one's embodied sense of belonging, a home far from home.

The newest versions of hand-knotted carpets, currently made mostly in refugee camps in Pakistan and Afghanistan, are "war carpets" that display the picturesque view of smart-weapon technology and expose a techno-romantic surface peacefully juxtaposing militaria with the landscape. They are replacing flowers, gardens, trees, and clouds with images of modern weaponry, such as tanks, rifles, grenades, helicopters, drones, and other technologies of war, as their key motifs. They aestheticize war, displaying fetishized weapons with magical powers to destroy both nature and the culture.

Like a computer screen, the carpet at the loom is a site of both visualization and virtuality, as it becomes a garden, a geometrical abstraction of shapes and symbols, a field of flowers and animals, an asymmetric or symmetric display of colors and shapes, a paradisiacal view simulating the actual into the virtual, or even a dystopic landscape covered with all kinds of weaponry. The weavers' digital juxtaposition of the artistic, the technical, and the mathematical creates webs of connections between the past and the present, the technical and the artistic, and the collective and the individual to bring the corporeal together with what will live for a *longue durée*. The weaver's body locates near the loom and arranges, aligns, and weaves together a multitude of different colored knots. The loom functions as a computer screen displaying the carpet while concealing the body. Such reticence precludes the panoptic intrusion of the industrial gaze as the weaver puts into action the design and shows the power to disarray and to disorder. Thus, the rug becomes a source of both anxiety and desire. The centrality of vision is interrupted at any moment as touch, sound, and memory take center stage, exposing the embodied experience of weavers-artists-creators as subjects situated in time and space with the ability to instigate and shift "the order of things." ∞

ABOUT THE AUTHOR *Minoo Moallem is a professor of gender and women's studies at the University of California, Berkeley. She is the author of* Between Warrior Brother and Veiled Sister: Islamic Fundamentalism and the Politics of Patriarchy in Iran *and has contributed to numerous books and periodicals on the subjects of religion, culture, film, and art. Her digital project* Nation-on-the-Move *(2007) was published in* Vectors Journal, *and her newest book,* Persian Carpets: Nation as a Transnational Commodity, *is forthcoming from Routledge in 2018.*

Hamra **Abbas**

{ B. 1976, KUWAIT }

HAMRA ABBAS GREW UP in Kuwait and Pakistan, learning from an early age to recognize and adjust to new customs, languages, and cultures. In recent years she has lived and worked in numerous other countries around the world, honing her adaptability as a traveler and nurturing an inherent appreciation for cultural heritage and differences. Her work showcases her interest in deep-seated traditions—particularly those related to religion—encompassing performance, sculpture, photography, painting, and installation; she often employs a variety of media in sequence on a single piece, effecting stages of mediation that represent the individual and collective filters through which customs and rituals inevitably pass. She classifies herself as an observer, engaging and empathizing with closely held beliefs while deliberately refraining from passing judgments.

For *Sanctuary*, Abbas created a design based on her 2016 work *One Rug, Any Color*, which aggregates mass-produced prayer rugs she purchased on Amazon.com. As the title suggests, she discovered a single design—featuring the Kaaba, the cubic structure that represents the most sacred site in Islam—available in a wide variety of colors. The ubiquity of the colorful, Kaaba-emblazoned rug in a global, digital marketplace, and the artist's presentation of a partial, slightly askew sampling of the rug's incarnations, highlight the spectrum of perspectives and experiences that exist in relation to religion, devotion, and faith—as Abbas notes, "diversity, variety, and difference within the idea of unity."

Adel **Abidin**

{ B. 1973, IRAQ }

BORN IN BAGHDAD, Adel Abidin currently divides his time between Finland and Jordan—an arrangement that finds him constantly straddling cultures and considering his identity through the eyes of those around him. Abidin's artworks become outlets for his reflections on ethnicity, citizenship, international relations, global crises, and personal responsibility. They are thoughtful and provocative, wry and unsettling, and always exquisitely rendered, whether he is working in sculpture, film, sound, drawing, or installation. Abidin's fluency with media affords great leeway in executing his ideas, allowing him to utilize the most affective combination of elements for each piece.

His design for *Sanctuary* comes from a 2017 relief sculpture titled *Deployed*. Based on a photograph of soldiers en route to a military assignment, the work explores his musings about individual soldiers' feelings as they head to battle: Are they afraid, worried, determined, hopeful as they move into the unknown? The uncanny similarity to images of crowded train cars and boats transporting political prisoners and refugees prompts correspondent thoughts about these displaced people. Abidin's composition concurrently reveals the difficulty in reading the individuals—humanizing each soldier or refugee—and seeing them as real people with relatable personal experiences. Here, the soldiers' expressions and gestures are elusive; their bodies and helmets meld together in a monochromatic sea. Yet the classical perspective and central vanishing point draw viewers into the scene, inviting a pause on each figure and urging contemplation of each soldier's story.

Arwa **Abouon**

{ B. 1982, LIBYA }

LIBYA-BORN, MONTREAL-BASED artist Arwa Abouon's works explore her experiences in the murky borderlands between Eastern and Western cultures. Through beautifully composed photographs and films, she presents compassionate, tender portrayals of individuals—often herself and her family—who straddle this cultural line as Muslim immigrants living in a Western country. "The themes addressed in my works stem directly from my life experience as a female artist living and working between cultures, and yet the aim is to show how a single person's 'double vision' can produce images that possess much wider social and political effects by collapsing racial, cultural, and religious borders," Abouon says. "In other words, the images which are seemingly autobiographical in nature move beyond mere autobiography."

Her design for *Sanctuary* invokes the aesthetic simplicity displayed in her recurring graphic illustrations. The rug, titled *The Pentagon-Shamsiya*, presents a traditional Islamic geometric pattern formed with the repeated image of the iconic US Defense Department headquarters, known as the Pentagon. "The integration of the architectural plan of the American Department of Defense into the wider overall aesthetic of Islamic pattern proposes an interesting critical rereading of both," Abouon says. "Revealing similarities between cultures and/or a possible space for Islam within American society is intended to evoke the Koranic verse from the Surah al-Hujurat (49:13), putting forth that nations and tribes were created to come to know and learn from each other."

Shiva **Ahmadi**

{ B. 1975, IRAN }

CURRENTLY BASED in Northern California, Shiva Ahmadi grew up in Iran during the periods of intense political unrest that surrounded the Iranian Revolution and the Iran-Iraq War—events that shaped her life experiences and, along with the Arab Spring, continue to inform her art. Whether rendered on paper, in animation, or, here, with textiles, her works captivate with their exquisite details and otherworldly atmosphere. The elaborate decoration of traditional Indian, Persian, and Turkish miniature painting influences both her style and subjects, with religious and mythological characters populating compositions marked by rich colorations and spontaneous gestures from sprinkles of paint, grains of rice, and hair. But sinister elements haunt even her most playful and serene scenes.

Ahmadi's contribution to *Sanctuary* features a Buddha-like character seated on a lotus throne. But unlike traditional depictions of the spiritual leader, Ahmadi's figure is defaced, bloodied, and perched precariously on a tangle of briars. Instead of Buddha, the enlightened teacher, the artist presents a mere mortal struggling to balance the weaponry of warfare, which could teeter out of hand at any moment. Ahmadi continually probes the confluence of Eastern and Western cultures, and the notion of unpredictable threats that often hide in plain sight. She asks viewers to look beyond the surface and consider the implications of our choices and actions, and she reminds us of the fine line that separates peace and destruction.

Ai Weiwei

(B. 1957, CHINA)

AI WEIWEI'S EARLIEST YEARS were shaped by political oppression, as his family was sent to a forced labor camp and, later, into exile by the Chinese government as punishment for perceived transgressions by his father, a celebrated poet. Ai embraced art and its potential for making social statements as a young man, spearheading a formidable, 40-year career as both artist and activist—a combination of roles that he sees as a professional responsibility. "As an artist, my work is always trying to deal with aesthetics and at the same time moral and social conscience," he explains. "I think this is a duty of artists: to connect [themselves] to social change, to bear the responsibility to be part of the change."

Ai's *Sanctuary* design borrows imagery from a 360-degree wallpaper installation created for the Smithsonian's Hirshhorn Museum and Sculpture Garden, titled *The Plain Version of the Animal That Looks Like a Llama but Is Really an Alpaca*. The work creates a pattern from graphic representations of chains, handcuffs, surveillance cameras, and the Twitter bird—allusions to restrictions on freedom generally, as well as Ai's own battles with government detention, authoritarianism, and censorship. "The misconception of totalitarianism is that freedom can be imprisoned," the artist has said. "This is not the case. When you constrain freedom, freedom will take flight and land on a windowsill."

John **Akomfrah**

{ B. 1957, GHANA }

JOHN AKOMFRAH INHERITED an affinity for political activism from his Ghanaian parents, embracing social causes as a young man and becoming a founding member of the Black Audio Film Collective, which set out to provide a forum for new voices amid discussions around postcolonialism and black identity in Great Britain. Through the collective, he launched an acclaimed career in visual arts, frequently exploring issues related to the black diaspora in the United States and Europe.

His rug design for *Sanctuary*, titled *The Cave*, is a kaleidoscopic pattern based on prehistoric paintings from Argentina's Cueva de las Manos. "Inside these interlocking caves are some of our first signatures of an idea," Akomfrah explains. "They are the ghost traces, the carbon footprints of us reaching for and attaining something very powerful, something very long lasting and very human. They are some of the first manifestations of a now near-universal human sense: the idea of an enclosure—marked by a sign of our presence—as a space of benediction, of sanctuary. What the caves tell us, too, is . . . our yearning for sanctuary, both as symbolic evocation as well as real knowledge of an actual place, [is] one of the oldest human yearnings. It's as old as our sense of home, as enduring as our grasp of time, as defining as our sense of mortality."

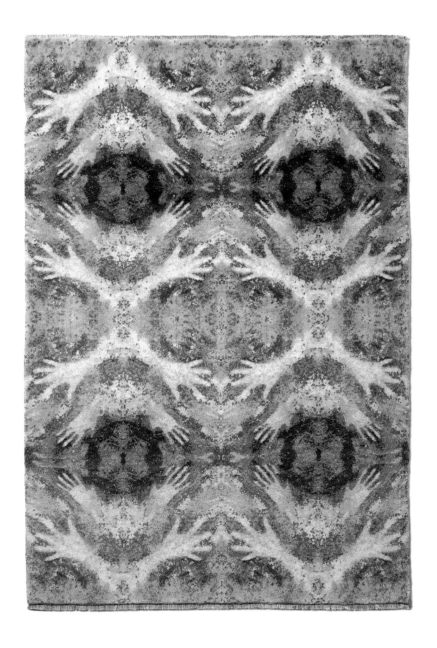

Ammar al-Beik

{ B. 1972, SYRIA }

AMMAR AL-BEIK'S WORK directly addresses the ongoing political strife in his home country of Syria, as well as the ever-escalating violence and oppression there. Art, al-Beik believes, can be a potent form of rebellion, allowing the artist to express feelings and ideas that the audience can absorb viscerally, not just intellectually. His work is subtly narrative, manifested primarily in mixed-media installations, photographs, and films, for which he has gained particular renown. (He is the only artist to have represented Syria twice in the Venice International Film Festival.) In 2014, when he relocated from Damascus to Berlin, the focus of his work shifted to notions of exile and displacement, mirroring his own experiences as a refugee.

His untitled design for *Sanctuary* is a brash critique of US President Donald Trump and Syrian President Bashar Al-Assad. "A carpet is a free space to create symbols that haunt us," he says. "When [carpets are] lined up side by side in houses of worship, [their] energy is magnified. They deliver messages of love, and often of pain and loneliness." The word *animal* appears in both Arabic and English, borrowing Trump's much-publicized criticism of Al-Assad to label both leaders; a chemical weapon hovers overhead "like mistletoe leading to a toxic kiss." "This is my first carpet—my political manifesto, my summary of confusion—but it will not be the last," al-Beik asserts. "There will be another: a manifesto of love, a magical carpet beyond the limits of time."

Diana **Al-Hadid**

{ B. 1981, SYRIA }

THOUGH DIANA AL-HADID was born in Syria, she asserts that her upbringing in the American Midwest is at least as influential on her work as her family's ethnic heritage. In fact, she draws inspiration from a broad array of art historical and cultural sources, from Roman antiquities to Renaissance masters to contemporary architecture and engineering. Al-Hadid is fascinated by perception—in literal, technical, and theoretical senses—and she toys with visual perception by exploiting the relationship between her works and the surfaces around them, allowing light and shadow to influence what the viewer sees.

Al-Hadid's rug design is based on her 2016 wall sculpture *The Extinction*, which references the oldest known hand-knotted rug, the Pazyryk Rug, woven in the fifth century BC, most likely in Persia. A three-dimensional piece masquerading as a painting, *The Extinction* was created by meticulously layering polymer gypsum, fiberglass, steel, plaster, aluminum leaf, and pigment to construct a lattice-like structure whose appearance changes subtly but palpably as the viewer's perspective shifts. The work is a study in contradictions: strong materials expressed as a fragile object, a complete piece that looks to be an eroded remnant of something else, a heavy mass that seems to float in midair. These physical characteristics are manifestations of conceptual underpinnings that extend beyond art to the human experience, including notions of displacement, belonging, and how context can influence meaning and identity.

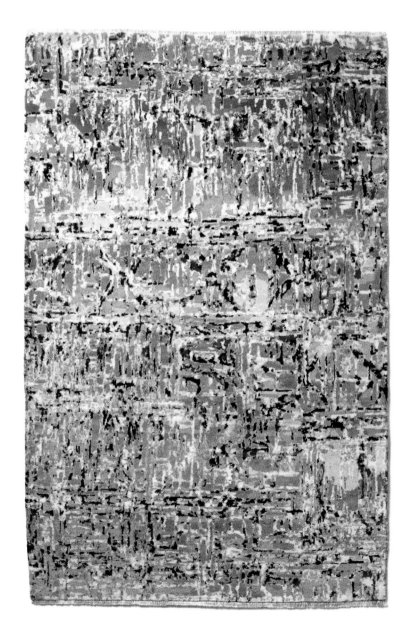

Tammam **Azzam**

(B. 1980, SYRIA)

MUCH OF TAMMAM AZZAM'S WORK reflects on themes of displacement, destruction, and the daunting task of rebuilding cities, cultures, and lives. Born in Damascus, Azzam saw his city crumble around him amid growing political conflict, fueling his current migratory existence and shaping his art practice. Working across a variety of media, he incorporates his experiences as a refugee and a native of a war-torn land both to address his personal struggles over such senseless loss and to broaden the impact of these experiences for a global audience. His viral *Freedom Graffiti* digitally marries imagery from Western masterworks with bombed ruins in Syria; his *Storeys* paintings depict war-ravaged cityscapes devoid of place-specific features; and his most recent *Paper* series introduces paper collage as a means of heightening a visceral sense of fragility and fragmentation.

Azzam's paper collages are the basis for his untitled *Sanctuary* rug design. The concept of sanctuary is particularly resonant for him; he has used the word to describe his former studio in Syria, which was a refuge from the turmoil he witnessed and experienced before fleeing in 2011 to Dubai and subsequently relocating to Germany. The Syria of his memory and the places he held sacred are now gone, forcing him to find solace, comfort, and safety in new locations, new experiences. "My family left with nothing, just our suitcases. We started a new life from zero," he has said. "But . . . I know I am one of the lucky ones."

Sandow **Birk**

[B. 1962, UNITED STATES]

DETROIT-BORN and Southern California–raised Sandow Birk works in the aesthetic tradition of history painting, turning his lens from the triumph of rugged individualism and American expansionism to contemporary struggles related to race, ethnicity, religion, and law enforcement. Birk puts uncomfortable histories and politically divisive social issues center stage, exposing the hypocrisy, double standards, and bigotry that still fester in a country that prides itself on global leadership and moral authority. His detailed compositions are rife with symbolism, from art historical references to the use of corporate logos. Recontextualizing masterpieces like Dante's *Inferno* and Emanuel Leutze's *Washington Crossing the Delaware* with modern settings and language, Birk dredges up past national wrongs that have been suppressed or forgotten, and points to how much work remains to be done in the quest for equal protection under the law.

Birk's rug design draws from his 1999 painting *Northwards the Course of Immigration Makes Its Way*, which he based on Leutze's 1891 painting *Westward the Course of Empire Takes Its Way*. The Leutze work, which hangs in the US Capitol building, celebrates classic American ideals—bravery, enterprise, self-sufficiency, pursuit of promise—depicting pioneering adventurers navigating a treacherous but beautiful Western landscape. Birk's intrepid travelers similarly strive for a brighter future, but as suggested by the menacing maw of border fencing and a brutalizing pair of armed guards in their path, the obstacles they face are more malicious, and the rewards far less certain.

Mohammad **Bozorgi**

{ B. 1978, IRAN }

MOHAMMAD BOZORGI WORKS within the rich tradition of Arabic and Persian calligraphy, bringing a contemporary sensibility to an ancient art. A biomedical engineer by training, he is precise and methodical in his approach, but his artistry shines through his innovative applications of calligraphic text; his elegant interweaving of ribbonlike characters; his bold use of color; and his adherence to principles like symmetry and repetition, which characterize Islamic art. Bozorgi's unique vision builds on more than 10 years of training with the Society of Iranian Calligraphers, through which he mastered a number of traditional calligraphic forms. The words he chooses for his compositions are as important as the designs, illuminating ideas and imbuing each piece with greater depth of meaning.

His *Sanctuary* design, titled *I am nobody, who are you?*, challenges the notion that war can strip one of identity by cutting ties to country, family, and friends. "Our homeland is in the hearts of those who love us," Bozorgi asserts. "If we have no peace, it is because we have forgotten that we belong to each other." The Arabic words for "He is God" loop across the composition, revealing a brightly hued palette emerging in a fractured field of black. "The artwork examines the destroyed roots, distracted hearts, and ruined world, but some colors in my design show the hope," the artist says. "Just for a few moments, put yourself in my place—can you feel me? We should live together. There is a light at the end of the tunnel."

Jamal **Cyrus**

{ B. 1973, UNITED STATES }

JAMAL CYRUS is a Houston-based artist whose solo work expands on the visual and performance art he developed as a member of the collective Otabenga Jones & Associates, a group of young African American artists who fashion multidisciplinary works aimed at honest and empowered portrayal of the black experience in the United States. Cyrus's artistic investigations are rooted in history, reexamining archival documents to expose narratives of suppression and oppression, and modifying everyday objects—most notably, musical instruments—to craft potent statements on the tricky business of cultural blending.

Cyrus's *Sanctuary* design, titled *X-plane*, explores the notion of sacred ground. It begins with a rubbing the artist made of the sidewalk outside New York's Audubon Ballroom, a cultural monument from early 20th-century Harlem and the place where black rights leader Malcolm X was assassinated in 1965. Cyrus overlays the rubbing with imagery of the first page of Malcolm X's FBI file, an unremarkable institutional form displaying only bits of code and procedural information, and marred by redactions. The artist likens the geometric structure of the form to a building plan, explaining, "From this perspective the document becomes the representation of a three-dimensional space—in this case an archive, a reservoir of information, knowledge, and possibly enlightenment; a place where reading is done ritualistically, and new insights beyond the two-dimensional plane are revealed."

Ala **Ebtekar**

{ B. 1978, UNITED STATES }

ALA EBTEKAR WAS BORN in Berkeley, California, to Iranian activist parents. From an early age, he developed what he describes as "a deep, cosmic sense of identity and a sensitivity toward in-between-ness," which nurtured his interest in the differences and overlap between divergent cultures. He has traveled widely, studying Iranian pop culture and poetry, and contrasting their imagery, symbols, and metaphors with those that surrounded him growing up in the United States. His resulting spiritual and artistic explorations involve an idealized, other-worldly realm beyond the temporal human condition, as well as disquieting notions of identity and complicating cultural differences.

Symbolically, the arch of a doorway spans time and history, marking the transition between the earthly and divine, whether in architecture, illuminated manuscripts, or carpet designs. Eleventh-century Persian theologian, philosopher, and mystic Al-Ghazzali likened this division to two gates in the heart: one opening outward to the material world, one opening inward, to inspiration. For his *Sanctuary* design, titled *Makan* (*a sense of place*), Ebtekar incorporates arches, windows, and views of the cosmos, working with a 15th-century illumination of a divan by Persian poet Hafez and an image captured by the NASA/ESA Hubble Space Telescope's Advanced Camera for Surveys (ACS). Says the artist, "The piece provides a contemplative space where the personal psyche can connect with the cosmic spirit, where the earthly and the celestial can meet, and where ancient tradition can intersect with imaginings of the future."

Marcos Ramírez **ERRE**

{ B. 1961, MEXICO }

OFTEN CLASSIFIED as a "border artist" for his visually striking and conceptually ambitious works related to US-Mexico politics and culture, Marcos Ramírez ERRE has a more expansive reach than such categorization implies. His creations in media as diverse as murals, sculptures, films, and installations invoke a visual language that's accessible in its familiarity—eye charts, logos, monuments, mythological symbols, everyday consumer objects—to address issues often mired in social controversy. "I get inspired by society—their problems," ERRE says. "I react to current social and political events and the news."

A native Mexican who moved to the United States as a young adult, he quite naturally gravitated toward issues related to his two homes, from Mexican alliances with foreign oil companies to the United States' accession of vast expanses of Mexican land. His investigations into identity, community, and a sense of belonging are fueled by his own experiences as an immigrant but not limited to them; the borders he examines are more broadly economic, cultural, and aesthetic. Like all of his works, his *Sanctuary* design is aesthetically straightforward but conceptually complicated, acknowledging an era when access to information is more widespread than ever but questions of accuracy taint its consumption and reinforce audiences' existing perspectives rather than bridging new ones. Writing about the rug, ERRE notes, "Most of the time you have to descend into the darkest voids to be able to mine for the most precious prizes."

Brendan **Fernandes**

{ B. 1979, KENYA }

MUCH OF BRENDAN FERNANDES'S WORK takes on questions of authenticity—as related to cultures, civilizations, objects, identities, and experiences—and how perspective influences what is deemed authentic. Born in Kenya of African and Indian descent and having immigrated to Canada, Fernandes has firsthand experience navigating issues of ethnic and national belonging, the geopolitical legacies of colonialism, and issues of queer identification. "My work explores the thesis that identity is not static, but enacted," he says, "challenging accepted ways of thinking about what it is to have an 'authentic' self."

Fernandes's design, created in collaboration with artist Nontsikelelo Mutiti and titled *In Trust*, explores the social and political implications for people living with HIV/AIDS, as well as the broader threats to the freedoms of queer people in the current US political climate. The rug's pattern is based on traditional West African batik, with roses defining the contours of a fallen human body—an emblem of both oppression and resistance. The geometric latticework is formed by PrEP pills—medication used to help prevent the spread of HIV—calling attention to the drug's influence on queer behaviors and perceptions, including the alternating views of queer sex as a danger and a sanctuary. The ritual of taking the pills becomes a form of "daily prayer" that links those at risk of HIV infection to other groups of outsiders, such as immigrants and Muslims, who are depicted by the Trump Administration as threats to its citizenry and the American way of life.

Ana Teresa **Fernández**

{ B. 1981, MEXICO }

BAY AREA–BASED ANA TERESA FERNÁNDEZ operates at the inter-
section of social activism and politics. Working in a broad range of
media—including performance, painting, installation, sculpture,
and film—she challenges viewers to examine cultural biases, contradictions, and stereotypes, as well as public policies that trigger,
reinforce, and exploit them. She regularly takes on issues of gender
and sexuality, inequality, and oppression, often crafting images of
women in body-conscious, feminine clothing performing physical
labor. In recent performances at the US-Mexico border, she paint-
ed (wearing a cocktail dress and heels) sections of border wall to
blend with the sky, creating the illusion that they had vanished.

Her rug design, titled *Erasure*, showcases a work from a new series
of the same name for which the artist documented a performance
of erasure: painting her body black with thick acrylic paint in front
of a black background. The resulting video and suite of signature
large-scale, hyperrealist paintings leave only glimpses of color—in
this case, a searing pair of eyes. Fernández performed this act of re-
moval and mourning in response to the 2014 disappearance and
presumed murder of 43 young male student-activists in Ayotzinapa,
Mexico. For the artist, this unconscionable act raises critical questions: "Whose life can be erased so quickly? Why are some sectors
of our community treated in such a disposable way? What do we
need to do as a society to be seen and treated equally, like valued
human beings?"

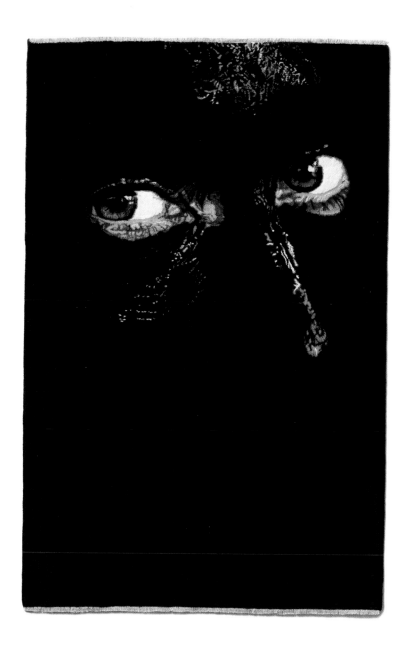

Nicholas **Galanin**

{ B. 1979, UNITED STATES }

GROWING UP IN SITKA, ALASKA, Tlingit/Aleut artist Nicholas Galanin developed a deep appreciation for the land and nature around him—affinities he channels into thoughtful artworks that engage contemporary culture in multifarious forms. He uses sound, images, and shapes to create critical ruminations on modern-day experiences, particularly cultural ambiguities, paradoxes, and contradictions. His flexibility in material and technique derives from the breadth of his concepts: the idea dictates the process. Whether working in sculpture, installation, photography, film, music, or performance, Galanin embraces beauty, and he presents incisive, thought-provoking analyses of identities and politics that evolve across generations in a multicultural society.

Galanin's *White Noise American Prayer Rug* references the pervasive global history of whitewashing or masking the uncomfortable, unsavory, and undesirable, as well as the xenophobic cacophony currently filling the American airspace. "This white noise is produced by a kind of whiteness based on more than complexion—based on capital, blind belief, and faith in itself, and fear of everything outside the lines it draws to enforce inclusion or exclusion under its laws," says Galanin. "This is the American prayer rug, a reflection of an image accompanying a droning sound to distract us from our own suffering, from love, from land, from water, from connection; there is no space for prayer, only noise."

Jeffrey **Gibson**

{ B. 1972, UNITED STATES }

JEFFREY GIBSON'S ARTWORKS are dynamic, colorful conflations of a host of cultural and aesthetic influences. In the context of his oeuvre, they read most obviously as outgrowths of his Native American heritage. But as the son of a US government official who grew up at posts across the globe, he also infuses each piece with bits of the multicultural episodes that shaped his identity, spanning club culture, fashion, and art history. An overarching theme in Gibson's work is "outsiderness," whether experienced as a member of a minority community, a foreigner, or a social outcast. "I think there's shame attached to being a part of a minority culture, and there's this desire to assimilate," he explains. "I don't want to expel who I am, because I'm not ashamed of it."

The brilliant hues and minimalist geometry of Gibson's design, titled *The Only Way Out Is Through*, showcase the overlap of Native artistry and 20th-century art movements like Minimalism and Op-art. The inclusion of text harks to his stated desire to give image to words. His chosen phrase has links to such varied sources as the Bible, Shakespeare, and Winston Churchill. (The latter famously said, "If you're going through hell, keep going.") Says Gibson, "For me the works have always been political. I'm oftentimes referring to past events, past cultural and political social movements, that there's still many questions surrounding how those things have unfolded. But there has been some level of resolve that I feel we can say is an achievement."

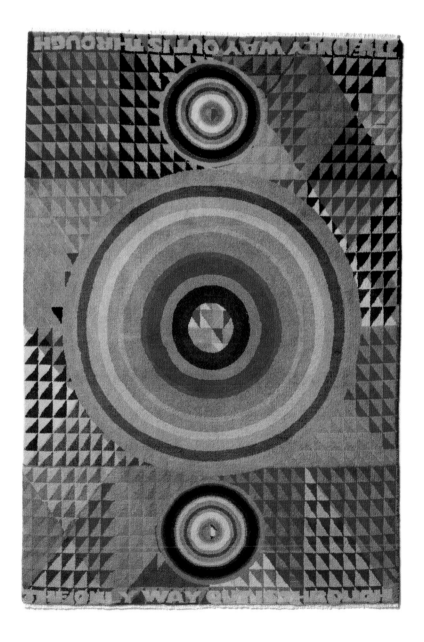

Sherin **Guirguis**

{ B. 1974, EGYPT }

THE INFLUENCES of both Eastern and Western cultures, thought patterns, and traditions are apparent in the work of Sherin Guirguis— a fitting amalgamation for an Egyptian-born artist who was swept up by the Arab diaspora at age 14. "Being a part of a diaspora does mean I'm living on the margins to some degree, and I have to say, I'm more comfortable in that position than ever before," she notes. "My work stems from that place—it deals directly with the attempt to find a language that describes that state of otherness that follows you wherever you are. I'm always home and I'm never home." Her works merge the spare geometry of Minimalism with the elaborate detail and gestural calligraphy of Arabic ornamentation, resulting in vibrant compositions that harmoniously interweave aesthetics and ideas that might seem conceptually at odds.

Guirguis's design for *Sanctuary* fills the plane of the rug with lush color, punctuated by stark geometric forms and sprawling rivulets of ink. Her deft blending of defined structure and unrestrained gesture—of formalism and unpredictability—showcases not only the multifarious imagery and techniques that shape her aesthetic but also the complexity, incongruity, and malleability that characterize the identities of displaced peoples. For Guirguis, disparate perspectives and inputs yield beauty, not conflict, generating something alchemical, wholly unique, and new.

Mona **Hatoum**

{ B. 1952, LEBANON }

MONA HATOUM'S EARLIEST MEMORIES are colored by a sense of dislocation. Born in Lebanon to Palestinian parents, she was ineligible for a Lebanese identification card—a gesture by the government to prevent assimilation. During a visit to London in 1975, she found herself stranded as war broke out in Lebanon. In the years since, she has settled in London, traveled extensively, and developed a dynamic art practice that explores human struggles related to political conflict, global inequity, and being an outsider. Materials are often the driving forces of her highly conceptual works, supplying symbolic subtext as well as a framework for realizing her ideas; as a result, her pieces take many forms, from photographs and performances to sculptures and installations. The uniting theme is an interest in points of friction in society.

Hatoum's rug for *Sanctuary*, *Untitled* (*rug*), is a material translation of an untitled paper cutout from 2009. Inspired by *papel picado*, Mexican "pecked paper" crafts, the work supplants the bright colors and traditional motifs—innocuous flowers, geometric designs—with drab armed soldiers, locked in opposing stances, surrounded by destructive explosions. Arranged in a circular pattern, the fragile paper figures call to mind the perpetuating cycles of conflict and war: with weapons raised, they are incapable of gaining understanding of the other or nurturing compromise, forever trapped in a doomed endeavor.

Susan **Hefuna**

{ B. 1962, GERMANY }

SUSAN HEFUNA'S WORKS inhabit the realms where potentially divisive perspectives—related to geography, ethnicity, religion, race, gender, culture—overlap and intersect. She grew up in a multiethnic context that moved among multiple countries, exposing her to a broad array of cultural and aesthetic influences. Instead of struggling to reconcile her identity with one culture or another—or defining her art by one influence or another—she elected to embrace the beautifully complex assortment at her fingertips, identifying herself as a global citizen and her works as celebrations and examinations of how we relate to differences in our world.

Based on her 2012 bronze sculpture *Be One*, Hefuna's rug showcases her conceptual interest in the *mashrabiya*, an Arabic architectural screen designed for privacy; the mashrabiya's intricate metalwork allows clear outward views while shielding a room's interior. "In my experience, most human beings are not able to see the world without a screen of social and cultural projections," Hefuna says. "The mashrabiya became a symbol that operates in two directions with the possibility for dialogue and awareness." She often incorporates language into her lattice-like sculptures and drawings, favoring simple phrasing that is open to interpretation. By presenting the words in durable media like metal and textiles, she gives them staying power, underscoring their significance for her and inviting audiences to ponder their meaning.

Thaier **Helal**

{ B. 1967, SYRIA }

THOUGH THAIER HELAL has lived in the United Arab Emirates since the 1990s, his Syrian home remains at the fore of his thoughts, works, and identity. In the years following the 2011 Arab Spring and the outbreak of war in Syria, the conflict and its collateral damage— destruction, displacement, injury, death, and ruin—have become the driving forces behind his large-scale paintings and assemblages. While some recent pieces use recognizable objects, motifs, and images, Helal's work is invariably abstract: he prizes abstraction's openness to interpretation, counting on viewers to bring their own experiences to bear on each piece. Incorporating materials like sand, glue, coal, and stones gives added dimension to the paint, allowing it to mound and crack in undulating ridges and furrows.

Helal's *Sanctuary* design, titled *Landmarks*, presents a detail from a recent work in a series of abstract landscapes that conjure topography more readily than scenery. By isolating a segment in close-up, he reveals its texture and depth, drawing viewers into a complex amalgamation of color, shape, and shadow that for him speaks of both hope and sadness. "I feel like after years of war, I prefer to paint the water and the earth. It says many things and holds many stories," he explains. "Nature has the most power—in the end it is that which will remain, not the war."

Shirazeh **Houshiary**

{ B. 1955, IRAN }

OVER THE LAST FOUR DECADES, London-based Shirazeh Houshiary has honed a career fueled by an embrace of spirituality, a fascination with materials, and an artistic agility that lends her work to a fluid assortment of forms. Part of a revered generation of artists to emerge on the London scene in the late 1970s, she continues to captivate audiences with her ever-inventive sculptures, installations, paintings, drawings, and films. At once ethereal and systematized, abstract and architectural, her works suggest a force beyond the human even as they probe decidedly human struggles.

For *Sanctuary*, Houshiary revisits a suite of layered etchings she made at STPI Singapore in 2016, titled *Migrants*. The subject of the works is the ubiquitous Singaporean rain tree, whose broad, balletic canopies dominate the landscape and serve as symbols of lush, natural beauty in the tropical island nation. The tree is not native to Singapore, or Asia, however; it is a transplant from the Americas whose alien status is all but forgotten. "To walk on the carpet is as if moving through the canopies of the trees. The overlapped multiple images . . . generate different perspectives where [the trees] can be viewed from above and below simultaneously," the artist says. "This carpet . . . is a statement about migration as a continuum in the process of evolution on our planet. Trees and animals have migrated across the planet long before humankind, and to stop migration is to stop life itself."

Alfredo **Jaar**

{ B. 1956, CHILE }

"I STRONGLY BELIEVE in the power of a single idea," says Alfredo Jaar, whose affecting, multifaceted artworks take on some of the most difficult events and conditions facing humanity. The Rwandan genocide, political oppression in his home country of Chile, and the continual death of migrants along the US-Mexico border are among the subjects he has mined over a career that spans more than three decades. Even when his subject matter is disturbing and un-settling, however, his works always include an element of beauty. According to Jaar, beauty is an essential part of every work because it is an essential part of life, even if global tragedies and injustices mask the beautiful with horror. While his highly conceptual works manifest in forms as varied as films, architecture, installations, sculptures, and photographs, one common denominator is their meticulous execution: each piece represents the crystallization of a fully formed idea whose impact grows as the idea is refracted through the lens of individual viewers.

His design for *Sanctuary*, titled *Requiem*, affirms his reputation for works of simple beauty that address complex sociopolitical issues. In this case, he reflects on a growing atmosphere of fear, mistrust, and oppression that seems to threaten human freedoms around the world. Lit candles have universal significance as symbols of life, rev-erence, memory, prayer, hope in mourning—they shine in vigils, fill altars, and commemorate unity. In his statement about the piece, he writes, "Light. More light. Light for these dark times."

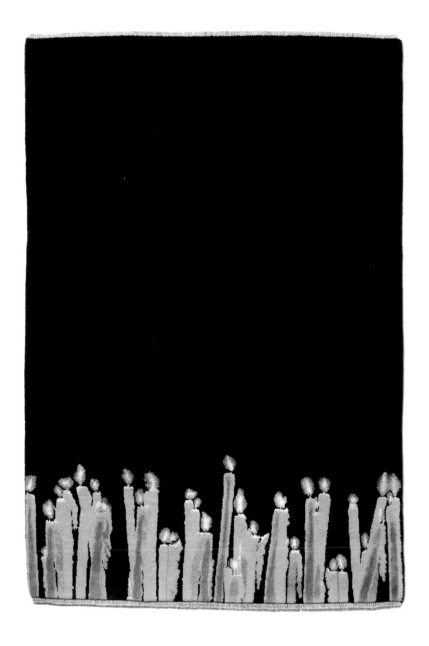

Emily **Jacir**

{ B. 1972, PALESTINE }

As POETIC AS IT IS political and biographical, Emily Jacir's work in-
vestigates movement, questions of translation, resistance, and silenced
historical narratives. Jacir has built a complex and compelling oeuvre
through a diverse range of media and methodologies. She explores
contrasting perspectives on events as filtered through collective, personal, and governmental lenses, examining the degree to which individuals' histories and rights are honored or denied. Her projects often
highlight the intimate details of her community, whether through
photographs of book inscriptions, a musical performance, or a sculpture embroidered with the names of decimated Palestinian villages.

Jacir's *Sanctuary* contribution presents an excerpt from her 2007
project *Material for a Film*, based on the life of Wael Zuaiter, the
first Palestinian intellectual assassinated by Israeli agents outside the
Middle East. The project rearticulated previously unknown ephem-
era from Zuaiter's life, in tandem with Jacir's own photographs,
writings, and interviews. Jacir simultaneously offers a self-portrait
as well as a portrait of a literary scholar, beloved son, and kindheart-
ed pacifist enjoying life amid artists in Rome. The text displayed
on the rug is a line from English poet Francis Thompson's "The
Mistress of Vision," which Jacir translated into Arabic and Italian;
Zuaiter quoted this line in the last article he wrote for the Italian
magazine *l'Espresso*. Some treatments are brightly foregrounded,
while others emerge slowly, raising subtle questions about political
dominance and the interrelationships of nations and cultures.

That thou canst not stir a flower
Without troubling of a star
دون أن تزعج نجما
لا تستطيع أن تحرك زهرة
That thou canst not stir a flower
That thou canst not stir a flower
Without troubling of a star
Without troubling of a star
Che tu non puoi agitare un fiore
لا تستطيع أن تحرك زهرة
دون أن تزعج نجما
That thou canst not stir a flower
Without troubling of a star
Che tu non puoi agitare un fiore
Senza disturbare una stella
دون أن تزعج نجما
That thou canst not stir a flower
Without troubling of a star
Che tu non puoi agitare un fiore
Senza disturbare una stella

Hayv **Kahraman**

{ B. 1981, IRAQ }

HAYV KAHRAMAN FLED IRAQ when she was 11. After living through two brutal wars, she and her family were granted passage to Sweden, where they lived as refugees. This personal history fuels Kahraman's artistic practice, through which she addresses the refugee's quest for identity, longing for an idealized heritage, and inevitable missteps as an outsider in a new land. Her canvases are strikingly beautiful, marrying the style of traditional Persian miniatures with a modern sensibility and often-jarring political commentary. Her figures strike classical poses, their gowns adorned with Islamic geometric patterns, yet they are accompanied by sinister elements, whether overt signs of exploitation or just the haunting serenity of their faces.

Kahraman's design for *Sanctuary* borrows imagery from her 2015 painting *Kachachi*, titled after a colloquial Iraqi term for "smuggler," which is scrawled in Arabic script across the bottom of the piece. She describes the scene as a childhood memory of her family hiring a smuggler to help them flee to Sweden. "When you are displaced because of war, you somehow get stuck in the past. I think this is specifically true when it comes to Iraqi refugees, because we are haunted by this sense of the glorious past—the cradle of civilization becomes something to focus on when your current situation is desolate. But as you flee to the West, you are obliged to assimilate," she says. "In this process I lost who I thought I was or could be. Introducing memory allows me to archive those lost histories."

{SANCTUARY}

Sanaz **Mazinani**

{ B. 1978, IRAN }

THOUGH SANAZ MAZINANI and her family left Iran for Canada in the late 1980s, the sights, sounds, and repercussions of the Iranian Revolution made distinct and lasting impressions, reverberating in her artwork today. Best known for her intricate, colorful panels and videos, Mazinani conjures Islamic geometric patterning, so pervasive in the Arab world, with pointedly contemporary subject matter and materials. From a distance, the patterns read as traditional ornamentation, but close inspection reveals them to be composites of meticulously organized and repeated images of weapons, explosions, protests, funerals, symbols of patriotism, suicide bombers, and pop culture icons sourced from the Internet. The juxtapositions are visually arresting and thought-provoking, beautiful in their kaleidoscopic arrangements but often disturbing in their content.

"Understanding the radical ways in which two people can perceive the same object with differing complexity is at the core of my investigation," Mazinani says. Her untitled *Sanctuary* design highlights the particular potency and significance of explosions, which have emerged as dominant visual tropes over her 12 years of examining news images for photographic montages. "For me, the symbolic likeness of an explosion stands in for an act of violence, but also for depictions of power . . . The explosion becomes a sublime entity to be feared and adored," she explains. "Here, the explosion's ability to obfuscate becomes a metaphor for politics, a symbol for the veils that simultaneously obscure and complicate reality."

Meleko **Mokgosi**

{ B. 1981, BOTSWANA }

MELEKO MOKGOSI'S PAINTING SUITES—classified as "chapters" in sweeping, multiyear projects—are grand and cinematic, enveloping the viewer in hyperrealistic mash-ups of historical, social, and cultural snapshots from southern Africa. The works are immediately captivating, thanks to their larger-than-life scale and Mokgosi's extraordinary ability to communicate both the impersonality of institutionalized oppression and the innate humanity of each individual on his canvas. Months of research go into each composition, informed by his own photographs of the region, news coverage, historical documents, and a scholarly appreciation of art history. His aim is to probe the difficult legacy of colonialism and the recurring rise of nationalism—in southern Africa and around the world. "[My subjects] are just ordinary people of southern Africa, and I'm invested in this space because I'm one of them," he says.

For *Sanctuary*, Mokgosi presents a recent excerpt from his project *Pax Kaffraria* (2010–17), from the chapter *Terra Nullius*. "Overall, this project examines the effects of xenophobia and national identification in southern Africa, and how this provides a context with which to understand the rise of nationalism in numerous countries across Europe and southern Africa," he explains. The work exposes the tendency to "otherize" those who fall outside dominant social hierarchies, to belittle and mistrust them, and to blame them for unrealized bliss—even if this bliss exists only in unattainable fantasy. When satisfaction is rooted in fantasy, it erects an obstacle impossible for an outsider to overcome.

Julio César **Morales**

{ B. 1966, MEXICO }

JULIO CÉSAR MORALES'S IMPROBABLE DEPICTIONS of migrants in hiding for cross-border journeys are poignant and disturbing even without the knowledge that they are based on actual documentation by US Customs and Border Protection. A native of Mexico who lives in the United States, Morales is moved by the plight of individuals so stricken with fear and desperation that they willingly risk safety and freedom for the chance to pursue a better life across the border. His work encompasses a broad variety of media—including music, sculpture, drawing, photography, video, and performance—to probe issues related to migration, labor practices, and underground economies, using artistic tools to engage audiences in a broader dialogue on human rights and welfare.

His rug design borrows an image from his ongoing *Undocumented Interventions* series, highlighting the harrowing conditions a young boy might endure for clandestine passage into the United States. Rendered in hand-drawn lines and watercolor, these works possess a beauty and ephemerality that belie the horrors they illustrate: men, women, and children tucked inside customized piñatas, suitcases, and vehicle dashboards that have been modified to accommodate and conceal living bodies. Ironically, while the "interventions" employed by migrants underscore a sense of despair and distress, they also highlight immigrants' ingenuity, determination, and dedication—qualities the United States purports to seek and prize.

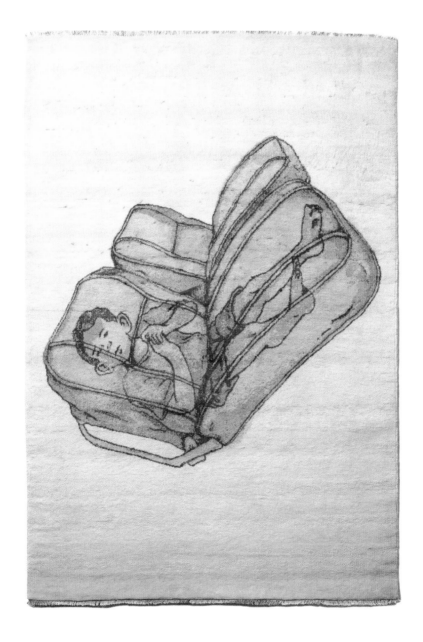

Aimé **Mpane**

{ B. 1968, DEMOCRATIC REPUBLIC OF THE CONGO }

A NATIVE OF THE CONGO who divides his time between studios in Africa and Europe, Aimé Mpane uses portraiture and sculpture to examine colonialism, political oppression, and racism in his homeland and beyond. "Living between two cultures and countries, the Congo and Belgium, my artwork is based on interactions between the north and the south and my reaction to stereotypes on Africa and black-skinned people," the artist says. "My artwork is fundamentally based on identity and wounds in the Congolese memory." Craftsmanship is central to Mpane's works; while he maintains a rough-hewn quality to his pieces, he is meticulous in his approach, carefully connecting matchsticks to form life-size figures, constructing mosaic-like wall hangings from hundreds of handcrafted tiles, and excavating portraits in layers of plywood.

Titled *Here we die*, Mpane's design for *Sanctuary* is based on one of his carved plywood portraits from a series of the same name. He creates these portraits with an ancient tool called an adze, which allows him to scrape away layers of wood and reveal his subject by reduction. Each panel is roughly 12 by 12 inches: the equivalent of a human head's surface area. "Because my work deals with problems of race and the stereotypes of black people, the three layers within four-millimeter-thick plywood make me think of the three layers within human skin," he explains. Despite the dark histories underlying his work, Mpane's portraits are not somber: his embrace of bright color lends an air of inextinguishable hope and promise.

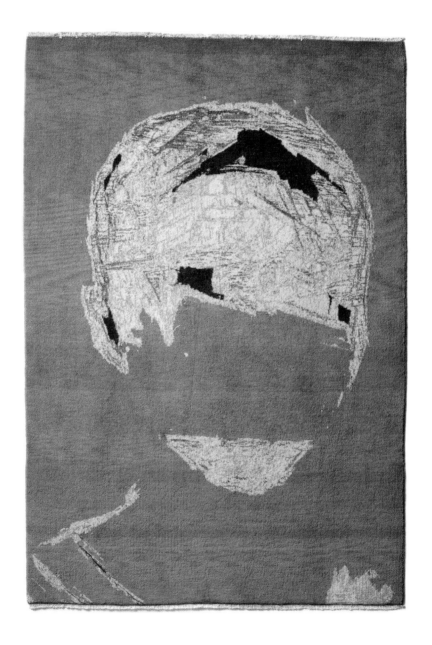

Aimé **Mpane**

97

Ranu **Mukherjee**

{ B. 1966, UNITED STATES }

MIGRATION, especially the journey of the refugee, is a topic Ranu Mukherjee returns to often in her artistic explorations. She follows the travels of nomads across cultures and ages, interspersing emblems from such diverse touchstones as Chinese mythology and Hollywood's Golden Age in order to conflate stories and histories from around the globe. Reflecting her disparate sources of inspiration, her works employ a wide variety of techniques and media, both traditional and contemporary—including ink, fabric, video, and sound—resulting in richly layered pieces that reward close inspection and contemplation.

For *Sanctuary*, Mukherjee weaves together the plight of modern-day refugees seeking safe harbor in the West, the political complexities that influence intercontinental travel, and traditional symbols of prosperity and peace in her rug design, titled *begin*. An ornate patterned ground veils the significance of overlaid lines: tracings from news images of refugees in the United States attempting to cross the border into Canada, fearing the harsh new US policies toward foreigners. Stripped of identifying characteristics, the figures emerge slowly, echoing the gradual process of cultural evolution as populations shift geographically, and emphasizing the timelessness of human migration. While the background pattern mimics the jacquard fabrics woven and worn in the cultures of many migrants, lending a humanizing element, the overlaid image of an olive tree, Mukherjee says, serves as "a kind of wish, to carry them to safety and peace."

Cornelia **Parker**

{ B. 1956, UNITED KINGDOM }

CORNELIA PARKER DRAWS FROM an eclectic arsenal of found objects, artifacts, and cultural history to create visually arresting, conceptually rich works that invite both introspection and outward assessment of the world around us. Through photographs, works on paper, sculptures, and installations, she brings to the fore episodes of societal violence and transformation, as well as transcendence, from class politics to racism to election campaigns to climate science. While specific events often serve as the seeds of her artistic ideas, she strives for ambiguity, allowing viewers the opportunity for individualized interpretations of what they see. She also enjoys the juxtaposition of the physical and the immaterial—of objects and the ideas or histories that animate them—often manipulating found objects so they can no longer function as originally intended; flattened brass instruments, crushed tea services, and exploded buildings require the audience's intellectual participation to give them renewed purpose. "I resurrect things that have been killed off," says Parker. "My work is all about the potential of materials—even when it looks like they've lost all possibilities."

Parker's design for *Sanctuary* is part of an ongoing body of work titled *Worry Lines*, in which she has photographed black safety netting subjected to tension. Here she calls attention to the netting's capacity for offering safety and protection, as well as its being a potential trap or snare. "It is a universal condition, that of vulnerability," she says. "We don't have solid, fixed lives; we're consistently in limbo."

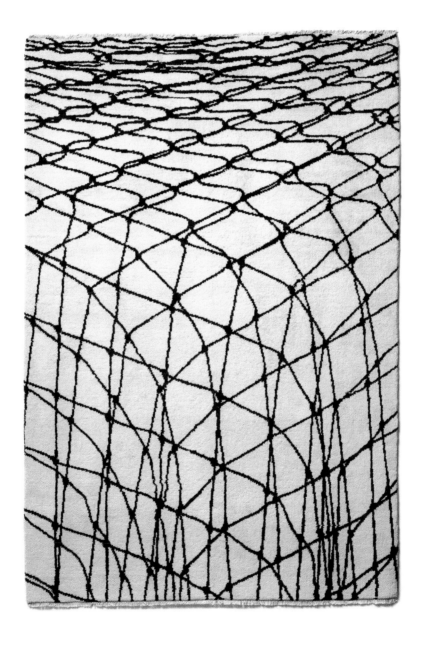

Rashid **Rana**

{ B. 1968, PAKISTAN }

MUCH OF RASHID RANA's acclaimed oeuvre encompasses imagery that is seemingly confrontational or political, but his primary interest is in disrupting conventional perspectives. His elaborate composite images, which effectively pixelate his compositions, sometimes comprise hundreds or thousands of smaller images; others rearrange elements of existing works in a gridded pattern to upend traditional viewing experiences. "Our experience of reality is a negotiation between the actual and the remote," Rana says. "The actual is close at hand—something one can experience directly with the body as the site of knowing. The remote is knowledge amassed indirectly, from diverse sources scattered across time and space," including books, the Internet, and collective knowledge, he notes.

Rana's design for *Sanctuary*, titled *Familial Unfamiliar 2*, is drawn from his ongoing *Transliteration* series. It features a Western masterwork juxtaposed with a contemporary photo of refugees adrift on open water and facing an uncertain future. His careful rearrangement of both images disorients the viewer and creates an alluring abstraction, but closer inspection exposes the contrasts between the painting's idealized gentry and the photograph's reluctant migrants. "By taking European paintings and rearranging their fragments, I'm trying to see the possibilities beyond that one particular image, and free them from a specific time and place," Rana explains. "By transliterating them, we liberate ourselves and see beyond their original contextual frameworks."

Miguel Angel **Ríos**

{ B. 1943, ARGENTINA }

MIGUEL ANGEL RÍOS'S PRACTICE provides a platform for the artist to examine issues of migration, including the often destructive and futile efforts to prevent and contain movement across borders. An Argentine native who fled to New York during his country's "Dirty War" in the 1970s, Ríos currently divides his time between studios in New York and Mexico City, affording a multinational experience that brings to the fore the challenges immigrants—particularly Latin American immigrants—face in the United States. His oeuvre includes sculpture, work on paper, photography, and installation, but over the last two decades, he has delved primarily into video, utilizing production methods and circumstances he describes as "difficult, dangerous, and impossible" to reinforce his symbolic narratives about human experience, violence, and mortality.

Ríos's *Sanctuary* design borrows imagery from his powerful 2015 film *Endless*. The film, which he shot over four months in Mexico, takes the viewer over and through narrow passageways lined by dense, thorny walls of *huisache*, Mexican sweet acacia. The trek between the brambles is ominous and threatening, yet remaining on the straight and narrow keeps the traveler safe. The overhead view—depicted on the rug—emphasizes the density of the walls, the darkness of the passage, and the relief of rising above the fray. "I make visible the violent moment in which we live, where we feel that life has no value," the artist explains. "It is competition, power, violence, and chaos. The viewer may choose to identify with the powerful or with the vulnerable."

Hank Willis **Thomas**

{ B. 1976, UNITED STATES }

NEW YORK–BASED Hank Willis Thomas takes on the United States' complicated relationship to race and ethnicity with unflinching directness, analyzing difficult chapters in American history and showcasing the stereotypes and biases that perpetuate racial inequities more than 150 years after the abolition of slavery. Thomas deftly channels his ideas across media, creating exquisite sculptures, photographs, paintings, and installations that seduce viewers with beauty and whimsy, and confront them with biting social commentary. Pop culture—particularly as revealed through branding and advertising—provides the visual fodder for much of his work, whether in the form of advertisements with product messaging removed, logos applied in unexpected places, or juxtapositions of contemporary tropes with symbols of slavery and oppression.

His *Sanctuary* contribution, titled *Keep the Faith Baby*, comes from a recent series invoking buttons and slogans from political campaigns and social movements from the last 50 years, removing them from their original context to allow audiences to reinterpret the messaging through a contemporary lens. Thomas remembers encountering a button bearing this particular wording as a child. The phrase, used by New York Congressman Adam Clayton Powell, originally served to communicate the hope and profound faith that fueled the American civil rights movement. "It may sound trite, but commercialism is the new religion. We are all believers. Even the most radical of us," Thomas has said. "It's not propaganda anymore."

KEEP
THE
FAITH
BABY

Uman

{ B. 1980, SOMALIA }

Uman's colorful abstractions are studies in contrast, and harmony. Her works bring together themes such as the overwhelming vastness of the universe and the intimate beauty of an individual's lived experience, using familiar ideas and imagery to expose and embrace fluidity in the realms of gender, nationality, and religion. The self-taught artist draws on her multinational upbringing across Africa, Europe, and North America, as well as her Muslim roots, incorporating calligraphic gestures from her study of the Koran, earth tones from her childhood in Kenya and Somalia, and the brilliant hues of sunsets in Upstate New York, where she currently resides.

For *Sanctuary*, she recasts a portion of her mural *The Universe*, which adorned the ceiling of a former studio space in New York City. The image is a colorful rendering of the Hubble Deep Field—a fractional photographic mapping of the constellation Ursa Major by the Hubble Space Telescope, compiled from more than 300 individual exposures—whose infinitesimally narrow view of the universe nonetheless captures an astonishing number of nascent, distant galaxies. "One among the infinity of worlds looking outward at the others—each unique and all part of the same universal mosaic," Uman writes of the Hubble perspective. "The universe—stretching to infinity, and now held in our minds."

Acknowledgments

When an organization works with artists around the world, in public spaces, in conjunction with the sites' overseers, that organization gets accustomed to logistical challenges. When an exhibition involves 36 artists from 21 countries, 50 artisans across Pakistan, and a historic building, the challenges can only be overcome by a shared sense of purpose, masterful teamwork, and the participants' unflagging commitment. I am extraordinarily grateful to all who made *Sanctuary* possible—first and foremost, the artists, who embraced the thesis and entrusted us with their ideas. Immense gratitude also goes to the team at ALRUG, including its network of artisans, who rose to the task of fabricating dozens of incredibly complex rugs on an ambitious schedule. This exhibition could not have been realized without the clear curatorial vision of Jackie von Treskow and the tireless multitasking of Alison Konecki, the brilliant design of Jennifer Burke, the wordsmithery of Anne Ray, the technical support of Ari Salomon, the media savvy of Florie Hutchinson, and the fund-raising prowess of Miegan Riddle. We are indebted, too, to Monica Herbert, Anne-Marie Litak, Shaghayegh Cyrous, Nik Sonfield, Kyle Smith, and our volunteer Art Guides for their invaluable assistance. Our gratitude also goes to our partners at Fort Mason Center for Arts & Culture, who were enthusiastic supporters from the outset. Special thanks go to our insightful and erudite catalogue contributors Rebecca Solnit and Minoo Moallem, cartographer Molly Roy, photographer Robert Divers Herrick, and Haines Gallery Director David Spalding, whose considerable efforts brought this publication to life. Finally, I would like to extend sincere thanks to Sheila Duignan and Mike Wilkins and to the Neda Nobari Foundation, without whose support the exhibition would not have been possible. —Cheryl Haines

This catalogue is published in conjunction with the San Francisco exhibition of *Sanctuary*, October 7, 2017–March 11, 2018. The exhibition is organized by the FOR-SITE Foundation with the support of Fort Mason Center for Arts & Culture and made possible by the generosity of our donors.

FOR-SITE STAFF

Cheryl Haines, Founding Executive Director

Jackie·von Treskow, Program Director

Alison Konecki, Communications and Development Manager

SANCTUARY RUG PRODUCTION

Mushtaq Ahmad, Shafiq Ahmad, Tanveer Ahmad, Zubair Ahmad, Fareed Ahmed, Khalid Ahmed, Mohammad Akhtar, Mohammad Arif, Mohammad Asghar, Mohammad Ashraf, Mohammad Asif, Nasreen Bano, Ghazala Bibi, Parveen Bibi, Rani Bibi, Razia Bibi, Mohammad Boota, Javid Faisal, Abid Hussain, Akram Hussain, Dillawar Hussain, Sabir Hussain, Sajjid Hussain, Shabir Hussain, Tariq Hussain, Yasir Hussain, Mohammad Imran, Mohammad Kashif, Abdul Khaliq, Zohaib Khan, Sajjid Mahmood, Raju Majeed, Tariq Matloob, Amjad Mehboob, Yaseen Mushtaq, Yasir Mustafa, Mohammad Nadir, Mohammad Qasim, Mohammad Ramzan, Abdul Rasheed, Mohammad Rizwan, Shan Sabir, Tanveer Sabir, Shahid Saleem, Mohammad Shaan, Mohammad Shahid, Mohammad Shahzad, Mohammad Shahzeb, Mohammad Tahir, Mohammad Tariq, Mohammad Yaqoob, Shan Yasin, Shehad Yasin, Mohammad Zeb

SANCTUARY CATALOGUE PRODUCTION

Designer: Jennifer Burke / Industry

Editor: Anne Ray

Photographer: Robert Divers Herrick

Additional artwork: pp. 11–17: courtesy ALRUG; p. 18: US Army, courtesy Golden Gate National Recreation Area Archives; pp. 30–31: Molly Roy. All rugs courtesy the artists, and p. 43: The Third Line, Dubai; pp. 49, 83: Lisson Gallery, London; p. 53: Marianne Boesky Gallery, New York; p. 57: Catharine Clark Gallery, San Francisco; pp. 59, 81: Ayyam Gallery, Dubai; p. 61: Inman Gallery, Houston; p. 63: The Third Line, Dubai, and Anglim Gilbert Gallery, San Francisco; pp. 99, 105: Gallery Wendi Norris, San Francisco.

TITLE PAGE Detail from Adel Abidin's rug for *Sanctuary*.

OVERLEAF Installation detail of *Sanctuary* at Fort Mason Chapel, San Francisco, October 7, 2017–March 11, 2018.